WHY DO THE RIGHTEOUS SUFFER?

JOHN MARINELLI

Why Do the Righteous Suffer?
Copyright © 2020 by Rev. John Marinelli
All rights reserved.
First Edition: 2021

Contact:
P. O. Box 831413
Ocala, FL. 34483
johnmarinelli@embarqmail.com

Cover and Formatting: Streetlight Graphics

No part of this book may be reproduced, scanned, or distributed in any printed or electronic form without permission. Please do not participate in or encourage piracy of copyrighted materials in violation of the author's rights. Thank you for respecting the hard work of this author.

TABLE OF CONTENTS

Preface	v
Introduction	1
Chapter One	3
Chapter Two	11
Chapter Three	18
Chapter Four	26
Chapter Five	40
Chapter Six	44
Chapter Seven	50
Chapter Eight	57
Chapter Nine	61
Chapter Ten	65
Chapter Eleven	69
Chapter Twelve	73

Conclusion 78
About The Author 83

PREFACE

I will answer the age-old question, "Why Do The Righteous Suffer?"

It is my understanding that there is a difference between the righteous and the unrighteous and therefore a difference in how God treats each group.

I will discuss the popular belief that God causes suffering either directly or indirectly.

Does God actually allow His children to suffer? All of this and more will be in question.

I will present 12 reasons why the righteous suffer and some suggestions on how some suffering can be avoided.

INTRODUCTION

I just hate to complain. I mean, I don't want to burden you with all of my problems. However, I have to tell someone and it might as well be you. You don't mind, do you? It won't take long.

My back is killing me. My knee is too and I get head aches all the time. I don't see that well anymore but I never did see great because of that awful brain hemorrhage when I was a baby.

I am somewhat depressed because folks are talking about me behind my back. I don't know what they are saying but it probably isn't good.

I think I have the flu or some other bug. I hope it's not cancer or another disease. I better get to the doctor before it gets really bad.

Why do I suffer so? I try to be good and go to church. I am not a bad person, am I? Why me Lord?

Do you fit into any of the situations above or do you have your own that plague you constantly?

The real question is, "Why do the righteous suffer?" But who are the righteous? How does a person become righteous?

The popular thought in the Christian world today is that if we live a righteous life we will always be healthy and without the troubles that other folks have that are not living a righteous life. Is this true or is it false?

CHAPTER ONE

Free Will & Suffering

The righteous suffer because, like every other human being, they are endowed by God with, "Free Will" Let me explain.

As per Genesis, chapter two, man was made or created in the image and likeness of God.

This image is described in Paul's letter to the Galatians, chapter five, when he tells the church that the fruit of the Spirit is Love, Joy, Peace, Kindness, Long Suffering, Gentleness etc. These are character traits that God possesses and shares with mankind.

The "Likeness", however, of God is in his ability to reason and make choices. God takes no prisoners into His kingdom. We choose to go and to be a part of what God is doing. That is called, "Free Will"

We have the free will to be like God. His likeness is seen

in our ability to choose our own destiny, do our own thing and be our own self…again this is, "Free Will."

The problem with free will is it was intended to elevate us up onto the same level as God so we could actually have fellowship with Him as an equal. That is not to say, as a god but as a being that can have an intelligent conversation with God. To do otherwise would make us to be no more than robots.

This relationship is seen in Genesis where the writer tells us that Adam walked with God in the Garden of Eden in the cool of the day.

Can you imagine their conversation? Maybe it was about creating other worlds or expanding the number of stars. Whatever it was, it was on God's level and Adam had the ability to be there. This was before he sinned and fell from God's glory.

You'll remember that God breathed into Adam, giving him the, "Breath of Life" and he became a living soul. That breath was the very life of God and was also what enabled Adam to walk with God on his level.

This, "Breath of Life" was also what was lost in Adam's transgression. He died spiritually and was no longer able to be on God's level. This same death passed on to all men for all have sinned, so Paul declares in Romans, chapter five.

What man didn't loose was his free will. He still had the ability to choose and shape his own destiny.

Take a look at today's society. In 2020 nine cities in the USA were ablaze with riots and civil disobedience. Homosexuals flaunted their immoral lifestyle; Mayors defunded police departments and told officers to stand down.

False religions were and still are trying to destroy the Name of Jesus and the Christian influence in the world. Morality is no longer the norm. Even the media supported evil and ungodliness.

Man's, "free will," and his subsequent choices fuel alcoholism, child abduction, prostitution, gang violence, and a lot more.

The Righteous Man

It is important to distinguish between the righteous and those that are not. Being a Christian or a member of a church or faithful to a particular religion does not make you righteous. Keeping a set of rules or adhering to a particular doctrine won't do it either.

We must go back to the Bible to understand the difference. Here's what Paul said to the believers at Rome during the 1st century.

"As it is written, There is none righteous, no, not one:" Romans 3:10

"For all have sinned, and come short of the glory of God;" Romans 3:23

"For the wages of sin is death; but the gift of God is eternal life through Jesus Christ our Lord." Romans 6:23

Paul is clearly saying that there is no one that is righteous; that all of us have fallen from or come short of God's glory and that we are all sinners with a death sentence on our heads.

He continues in chapter five telling us why. He says; *"Wherefore, as by one man (Adam) sin entered into the world, and death by sin; and so death passed upon all men, for that all have sinned:"* Romans 5:12

I am not saying that there is no difference between the righteous and the unrighteous because all have sinned. Before you declare me a heretic, listen to the rest of the story.

"For he (God) hath made him (Jesus) to be sin for us, who knew no sin; that we might be made the righteousness of God in him." 2 Corinthians 5:21

Jesus went to the cross at Calvary to die as a penalty for our sins. He was crucified, sacrificed as the pure "Lamb of God" as atonement for the sins of the entire world. This is the good news of the Bible. It is the gospel.

Now Jesus clarifies why he went to the cross. It was because of God's love for His highest creation, Man. Hear it for yourself.

"For God so loved the world, that he gave his only begotten Son, that whosoever believeth in him should not perish, but have everlasting life." John 3:16

Thus, the "Whosoever" of John 3:16, that believes in Jesus will have eternal life. This, "Whosoever" through faith in Jesus can become the righteousness of God.

Now God looks at us and sees His own reflection, one of righteousness, secured for us by Jesus. We no longer fall short of God's glory. We no longer have a death sentence over our heads. Instead, we have the promise of everlasting life.

So, the righteous man is the one that believes in Jesus and looks to Him as Savior and Lord.

What does this have to do with suffering? Well, when we, the righteous, suffer, it is not under the mighty hand of God. He does not take pleasure in His children's suffering, even when it is because of disobedience.

Our suffering happens, in many cases, because of bad choices as we exercise our, "Free Will." Here are some examples:

Situation #1…You decide to stop in at a local bar for a beer. You have more than you should and leave. On the way home you hit an older lady walking on the sidewalk and she is killed.

Blame… Who's to blame? Is it the lady for being too old? Is it the bartender for serving you more beer than you could hold? Is it God for allowing this situation to happen? Or is it you and your bad choice? We like to blame others for our faults. It just cannot be me.

Situation #2…I wanted to fit in with the other guys in my school so I start smoking. I smoked everything I could get my hands on because they did. It is now 10 years later and I am an addict, smoking Pot, Cigars, a Pipe and injecting Cocaine. Oh yeah, I also have lung cancer.

Blame… Who's to blame? Is it the manufacturers of cigars? How about the stores that sold the cigarettes? What about the crowd I hung out with that ran wild into the drug scene? Or could it be God's fault for allowing such stuff to be within my reach? Do you suppose it could be my choices, that is to say, little old me?

We could go on through a thousand situations but it will still come down to our, "Free Will" and making bad choices.

"Free Will" can be a blessing or not, depending on how we use it. I feel sorry for those that blame God. I hear it all the time, "Why is God punishing me?" or "Why did God allow this to come upon me?"

What's really being said is, "Why did God give me the ability to think, reason and make choices?" It is like saying that I am not qualified to make informed decisions or live life with a certain amount of self-control.

Remember, God wanted the best for mankind and gave

him a great advantage over all of his creation, the ability to reason and choose.

The problem is that now we have to live with those choices and most of us would rather blame someone else, even God, for the wrong choices we make.

So the righteous suffers as a result of their own, "Free Will" choices. Don't feel bad. So does everyone else. In this scenario, we are no different than the ungodly. However, we have a loving Heavenly Father that we can go to and ask forgiveness. He will work everything out for our good. Hear what the Bible says,

"And we know that all things work together for good to them that love God, to them who are the called according to his purpose." Romans 8:28

The ungodly do not have this promise. It is given to only those, "Whosoevers."

There is a Biblical truth we can hold dear. It is that God loves us. He is not out to get us or hurt us in any way. Even when we make bad choices and fall short, He is there to keep us on the path to glory.

"I AM" There

"I AM" There,
At the end of your broken dreams,
Before the sun rises over your day,
Prior to those tear-filled streams.

"I AM" There,
Down that road of despair,
When all appears to be lost,
And no one seems to care.

"I AM" There,
Over all of life's twists and turns,
When tomorrow is all but gone,
And when you are full of concerns.

"I AM" There,
Sayeth the Lord of Host,
To bring you hope and peace,
And the power of My Holy Ghost.

"I AM" There,
To be sure you make it through,
In the midst of every trial,
To bless your life and deliver you.

"I AM" There
Poem By: John Marinelli

CHAPTER TWO

Disobedience & Suffering

Disobedience is a denial of truth. It is a sin against light. It is not, "I didn't understand" or "I didn't realize" It is a deliberate rejection of what you know to be true.

Adam's transgression was not a misunderstanding. He could never say, I was not aware of God's direction." He knew the truth and rejected it. He went against all that his creator said and embraced a lie that was presented to him by Satan.

You'll remember in Genesis that God said to Adam, *"But of the tree of the knowledge of good and evil, thou shalt not eat of it: for in the day that thou eat thereof thou shalt surely die."* Genesis 2:17

The devil suggests to Adam that he will not really die but become like God. Here's what the devil said;

"For God doth know that in the day ye eat thereof, then

your eyes shall be opened, and ye shall be as gods, knowing good and evil." Genesis 3:5

Now, for the first time, Adam was challenged to believe God. Had God kept his eyes closed so he did not see evil? Was knowing good and evil the mark of being a god? Was Adam deficient in that he did not know evil? What was evil anyway? Is it really that bad?

We can see, "Free Will" in action and get a feel for what Adam might have been thinking. The truth is, God did not want His creation to experience evil. He created man, as an innocent being, pure and holy, in His own image.

There is a lot of stuff that God does not want us to experience. One is suffering at the hands of evil men or demons. Another is being led down a road of destruction by a lie that blames God for the work of evil forces.

What Adam didn't know was that God had already made him to operate in a Godly realm. He possessed all the attributes of God. He was created in the image of God and God's likeness was all over him.

We would say, "He was the spiting image of his dad," if we were talking about our son. He even had the power to subdue the earth and make it a Godly habitation.

Adam was fully equipped to accomplish all that God wanted him to do. But the devil put a doubt in his mind that said in effect, that Adam lacked the most essential quality to fulfill his destiny. That quality was to know or operate in evil. In other words, to operate on his own, outside of the influence of his creator.

The underlying deception was that God was holding back something that was good and needed for Adam to complete himself. This premise is false. It goes against the very character of God. Adam must have known that he could only find himself in God. But he rejected that truth and looked elsewhere for his identity.

We become as we think. Our thoughts direct our actions and govern our destiny. Hear what the scripture says.

"As a man thinks, in his heart, so is he." Proverbs 23:7

As A Man Thinks

I am as my thoughts are,
No matter what you say.
If I think good or bad thoughts,
That is what rules my day.

You cannot know me,
As I really am,
Unless I reveal my thoughts,
And become a transparent man.

You are no different than me,
Underneath all the fleshy show.

We all are as we continually think,
Some happy and others full of woe.

So think on the things in life
That brings out your very best.
And you will surely get better
And be able to finally rest.

Poem By
John Marinelli

So Adam's rebellion caused the course of his life to change and he became what was in his heart…Sinful. This is what happens to us when we reject God's destiny to rule over our own lives. We become what is in our hearts…egotistic, selfish, immoral, hateful, jealous, and a lot of other bad attitudes…and finally, we die as a result of our sinful actions.

Let's take a look at some Biblical disobedience and what shift in destinies that occurred.

First there is Jonah. You remember him, right? He was told by God to go to Nineveh and to proclaim God's judgment upon that wicked city.

Jonah knew that Nineveh was a very wicked city and ruthless, killing thousands to be the most powerful city in all the land. He ran from the Lord in fear of Nineveh, disobeying God's command.

Most everyone knows what happened, Jonah booked passage on a boat heading away from his divine destiny. Then he was tossed into the sea in a great storm to appease the gods and was swallowed by a great fish, most likely a whale.

His destiny went from seeing the mighty hand of God at work against a wicked nation to gasping for air in the belly of a whale. There is always a consequence to disobeying God.

Jonah did finally accomplish God's will. He called out to God from within the whale with a repentant heart and was heard. The whale was ordered by God to deposit Jonah onto dry land where he made haste to Nineveh.

Now let's look at the disobedient prophet in the Old testament that did not tell the truth to some folks about a certain word that God had given him for the people. He took money for his services and told them what they wanted to hear, not what God wanted them to know. So as the prophet was riding his donkey, the death angel stood in front of the donkey in the middle of the road with a flaming sword.

The prophet whipped the animal for stopping and finally God opened the donkey's mouth and he spoke to the prophet. It was then that the prophet looked up and saw the angel of death. Had he not repented, he would have been slain by the angel. His destiny was saved but not before he stood face to face with death.

One final example is the children of God that came out of the land of Egypt. Here they are in the wilderness heading for the, "Promised Land."

They saw 1st hand the plagues that God brought upon Egypt. They saw the red sea open so they could cross on dry land. They saw the armies of Egypt drown as the sea returned. They were 1st hand witnesses to the power of God.

However, when the 12 spies returned from the land of promise, ten of them said the people of the land were giants, men of renound. They openly said, *"We are like grasshoppers in their sight."* The people fell into fear and saw the residents of the land as having more power than God.

Their disobedience in not believing God kept them in a wandering state for 40 years in the wilderness. Every adult except Joshua and Caleb died in the wilderness. God waited for the next generation to accomplish His divine will.

The children of Israel started out on a journey with God to realize their long awaited destiny, the Promised Land. However, that destiny was lost and replaced with suffering and death.

When God speaks to you, listen and be quick to obey. He

has your best interest at heart. His way may be bumpy, in some ways even scary but in the end, the best thing that could ever happen to you. We don't want to end up wandering in the wilderness of life with no purpose of destiny.

And thine ears shall hear a word behind thee, saying,

> *This is the way, walk ye in it, when ye turn to the right hand, and when ye turn to the left.*
>
> *Isaiah 30:21*

CHAPTER THREE

Divine Providence & Suffering

So far, we have looked at suffering because of bad choices centered in our own, "Free Will" and suffering as a result of disobedience i. e. rebelling against God. It's time to take on the big one.

Is suffering a part of God's divine plan? In other words, does God initiate suffering, as part of His will for an individual? Before we tackle this question, let's look at suffering and some obvious sources.

Suffering comes in various forms. It can be as a result of racial hatred, sickness, religious persecution, war, politics, vengeance, guilt and a lot more.

Suffering can be strictly an emotional thing, just physical or both. If you are being tormented by broken dreams and thoughts from the past, you can hurt just as much as if a car hit you and broke your leg.

It was in God's divine will that Jesus suffered a horrible

death on the cross. John records Jesus as saying, *"God so loved the world that He gave His one and only Son, that whosoever believes in Him shall not perish but have everlasting life."* John 3:16

It was by God's direction that Jesus suffered. His death paved the way for the redemption of all mankind.

However, does that divine suffering open the door for us to claim a divine privilege when we suffer? I think not. Yet I hear all the time folks saying, "Well, it's just my cross to carry in God's divine will." Most of this is an excuse to cover up a lack of faith.

Didn't Jesus also say,

"For verily I say unto you, That whosoever shall say unto this mountain, Be thou removed, and be thou cast into the sea; and shall not doubt in his heart, but shall believe that those things which he saith shall come to pass; he shall have whatsoever he saith." Matthew 11:23

God does not give us a cross to carry around. Jesus did that for us. He carried our sins and suffering so we wouldn't have to. Hear what Isaiah said about that.

"But he (Jesus) *was wounded for our transgressions, he was bruised for our iniquities: the chastisement of our peace was upon him; and with his stripes we are healed."* Isaiah 53:5

Suffering for the sins of the world is different than our suffering as a result of an accident. We suffer under the trials of life every day. Paul tells us to count it all joy…listen

"Count it all joy, my brothers, when you meet trials of various kinds, for you know that the testing of your faith produces steadfastness. And let steadfastness have its full effect, that you may be perfect and complete, lacking in nothing." James 1:2-4 ESV

When then can we say that our suffering comes from God as part of His destiny? James tells us that God did not initiate the trials of life that we face but He does use them to mature us and establish us in the faith. He uses the circumstances for our own good. Paul tells us that we should already know this truth.

"And we know that for those who love God, all things work together for good, for those who are called according to his purpose." Romans 8:28 ESV

I know what some of my readers will say. What about Job? Why did God allow the devil to attack him? He was doing everything right.

The story of Job is really interesting. On face value, it certainly appears that God ordered suffering to come on Job through evil forces. However a closer study says just the opposite. Let's take a look.

The story goes like this. God said to Satan, have you seen my servant Job? Satan said in effect, you have a hedge about him so I cannot attack him. Read on from here.

"Hast not thou made an hedge about him, and about his house, and about all that he hath on every side? Thou hast blessed the work of his hands, and his substance is increased in the land.

But put forth thine hand now, and touch all that he hath, and he will curse thee to thy face.

And the Lord said unto Satan, Behold, all that he hath is in thy power; only upon himself put not forth thine hand. So Satan went forth from the presence of the Lord." Job 1:10-12

Satan wanted God to participate in evil by touching Job and destroying his world. The problem with that is God does not destroy. He builds up and comforts the weary soul.

Satan had no idea that it was Job's faith that created the hedge. He thought it was God's doing.

The real question is, will man praise God only when he is prosperous? Satan clearly says that the wealth and stature in the land was the hedge about Job. There is also an implication that Job's righteousness is linked to his wealth. Take it away and Job will no longer follow you.

In today's world, many Christians believe that prosperity is the sign of being in God's will. If you are not prospering, you are not in God's will. That's just not true.

Every man does not have the same destiny. God has a plan

for each of us and that plan can be very different for me opposed to you.

Satan was complaining that he could not get to Job but God tells him, *"all that he hath is in thy power;"* Satan has always had power over humanity. Listen to what the Bible says about him.

"But if our gospel be hid, it is hid to them that are lost: In whom the god of this world hath blinded the minds of them which believe not, lest the light of the glorious gospel of Christ, who is the image of God, should shine unto them." II Corinthians 2:3-4

He is called, "The god of this world" and he can blind the minds of those that do not believe. He has control over them to do evil in the earth. Not so with the righteous because they resist evil by faith.

"Be sober, be vigilant; because your adversary the devil, as a roaring lion, walks about, seeking whom he may devour: Whom resist stedfast in the faith, knowing that the same afflictions are accomplished in your brethren that are in the world." I Peter 5:8-9

Paul tells us that Satan or the devil roams the earth in search of one that he can devour. He has always been in the earth looking to steal, kill and destroy. He started with Adam and continues with every human being in every generation.

Job had no special privilege. His faith in God made the hedge and God honored it.

"But without faith it is impossible to please him: for he that cometh to God must believe that he is, and that he is a rewarder of them that diligently seek him." Hebrews 11:6

We, like Job, can resist and watch evil forces flee. Our hedge is our faith in the promises of God. We hook our faith to a promise and believe. Satan cannot break through it.

Job is a good example of Divine Providence. A simple explanation of divine providence is God's will. He is supreme and what he says goes.

"So shall my word be that goes forth out of my mouth: it shall not return unto me void, but it shall accomplish that which I please, and it shall prosper in the thing whereto I sent it." Read full chapter · Isaiah 55:11

So God does what He wants and nothing can prevent it. This is divine providence. Here's a more detailed explanation.

Traditional theism holds that God is the creator of heaven and earth, and that all that occurs in the universe takes place under **Divine Providence** — that is, under God's sovereign guidance and control.

According to believers, God governs creation as a loving father, working all things together for good.

When physical suffering and emotional stress continues it is easy to say, "Where is God" Why is He allowing this to happen?

So it was with Job when he kept calling for an audience with his creator. As others, including his wife, said, "Curse God and Die" he stuck to his guns for that audience with God.

When Job finally got his meeting with God, he received no explanation as to why things were happening, why he had to suffer or what. He did get healed, restored and blessed.

Sometimes we never can figure out why things happen. We are challenged by circumstances to hold on to our faith anyway and praise the Lord, knowing that He has our best interest at heart.

I want to offer one more example of Divine Providence. It is found in John 9:1-3

"And as Jesus passed by, he saw a man which was blind from his birth. And his disciples asked him, saying, Master, who did sin, this man, or his parents, that he was born blind? Jesus answered, Neither hath this man sinned, nor his parents: but that the works of God should be made manifest in him." John 9:1-3

Birth defects happen all the time. Blindness is only one of them. Did God actually cause blindness or was it just a part of the normal birth process of mishaps? We can look at it either way.

I think that the man was blind as a natural occurrence. However, I do also think that God used the circumstance to reveal His mighty power. Here's why I think this way.

It is against the character of God to bring suffering upon His own child. Now that is excluding rebellion like the children in the wilderness. But to be blind from birth and Jesus saying that no one caused it is a clear indication of divine providence. If no one caused it, that includes God.

The man received his sight because God chose him to reveal His power. He has also called us from darkness into light that we may see the glory of God. We were also blind from our birth, actually spiritually dead and had to be "Born Again." We, like the blind man, were chosen by God to show His power and great love.

"If we suffer, we shall also reign with him: if we deny him, he also will deny us:" 2 Timothy 2:12

CHAPTER FOUR

Unforgiveness & Suffering

Unforgiveness is another reason that the righteous suffer. As Christians, we are to walk in forgiveness at all times. However, I must clarify this truth so as to protect you from demonic attacks.

We should not be so quick to forgive openly. We can do so within our hearts but before we move openly to forgive, we need to know a few things. Let's take counsel from the Bible.

"Then came Peter to him, and said, Lord, how oft shall my brother sin against me, and I forgive him? till seven times? Jesus saith unto him, I say not unto thee, Until seven times: but, Until seventy times seven." Matthew 18:21-22

Notice that forgiveness is focused to, "My Brother", not those outside the commonwealth of faith.

Your unforgiveness keeps you tied to the other person as long as you do not let it go. It is still an unresolved conflict. However, my willingness to forgive you has freed me from any unresolved conflict. Here's why:

1. By forgiving you, I break the cycle of hate.

2. By forgiving you, I burry the hatchet that binds us together in conflict.

3. By forgiving you, I no longer hold conflict as my primary focus. I can move on to other things.

4. By forgiving you, I can look upon you with a new perspective that excludes hate.

5. By forgiving you, I am delivered from the attacks of the devil that seek to torment me in the situation.

6. By forgiving you, I cleanse my attitude from bitterness so I do not defile others around me.

7. By forgiving you, I eliminate the stress and related illnesses associated with dealing with an offense over and over again.

In order to forgive and be forgiven, some things have to be crystal clear. Consider these:

- The one being forgiven must acknowledge that he or she is responsible for the fault.

- The one forgiving must be willing to truly forget the fault, so much so, that it never again becomes the primary topic of thought or discussion. (I have a saying that helps me. It goes like this, *"Let's not go down that road again."*)

- The one forgiving must accept and acknowledge any wrongdoing he or she may have done during the conflict. It could be insults, throwing things or even a demeaning tone of voice.

- Both parties must forgive themselves. Often, the person at fault can never forgive himself or herself, even when the other has forgiven them and God has forgiven them.

Reasons To Forgive

We forgive because God has forgiven us. (Ephesians 4:32) We forgive in obedience to God. (Matthew 6:14-15; Romans 12:18) We forgive others to gain control of our lives from hurtful emotions. (Genesis 4:1-8) We forgive so we won't become bitter and defile those around us. (Hebrews 12:14-15)

The Parable of The Unforgiving Servant

"Therefore is the kingdom of heaven likened unto a certain king, which would take account of his servants. And when he had begun to reckon, one was brought unto him, which owed him ten thousand talents.

But forasmuch as he had not to pay, his lord commanded

him to be sold, and his wife, and children, and all that he had, and payment to be made. The servant therefore fell down, and worshipped him, saying, Lord, have patience with me, and I will pay thee all. Then the lord of that servant was moved with compassion, and loosed him, and forgave him the debt.

But the same servant went out, and found one of his fellow servants, which owed him an hundred pence: and he laid hands on him, and took him by the throat, saying, Pay me that thou owe.

And his fellow servant fell down at his feet, and besought him, saying, Have patience with me, and I will pay thee all. And he would not: but went and cast him into prison, till he should pay the debt. So when his fellow servants saw what was done, they were very sorry, and came and told unto their lord all that was done.

Then his lord, after that he had called him, said unto him, O thou wicked servant, I forgave thee all that debt, because thou desired me: Should not thou also have had compassion on thy fellow servant, even as I had pity on thee?

And his lord was wroth, and delivered him to the tormentors, till he should pay all that was due unto him. So likewise shall my heavenly Father do also unto you, if ye from your hearts forgive not every one his brother their trespasses." (Matt. 18:23-35)

This parable has at lest 5 good points to consider about forgiveness. They are:

1. We are Stewards of our Heavenly Father's stuff and must do things in accordance to His will, not ours.

2. Because our King (Jesus) showed mercy to us, we are to show mercy to others that are in our debt.

3. Failure to be like our King is to be wicked and causes us to fall out of favor with our lord.

4. What we do to others, God will do to us. If we are merciful, so is He and vice versa.

5. We are to, from the heart, forgive those that are indebted to us when they ask for mercy.

The parable reveals that Jesus is talking about one who was forgiven but would not forgive. The wicked servant heard the words of the debtor for mercy but ignored them.

This is the point of forgiveness. If you are not getting a plea for mercy with an apology, you do not have to jump right into forgiveness. That debtor needs to know he or she was wrong.

If you jump the gun, you open yourself to repeated abuse. God doesn't want you there.

Now, lets bring this home. If you were wrong, and you know you were, you need to clear it up ASAP. However, if you are right, hold you ground until you get an apology or other form of retribution.

"And his lord was wroth, and delivered him to the tormentors, till he should pay all that was due unto him. So likewise shall my heavenly Father do also unto you, if ye from your hearts forgive not every one his brother their trespasses." Matthew 18:34-35

Question…Who are the, "Tormentors," In the above verse?

Normally the bankrupt debtor was sold into slavery. But, apparently, in extreme cases, where concealment of assets was suspected, the defaulter was sent to prison until restitution should be made. Probably the imprisonment itself was regarded as "torment" and the "tormentors" need mean nothing more than jailers. Quote by Burton Scott Easton

Now God has jailers everywhere. They carry out the torment prescribed by law. Just ask a burglar that got caught and spent 3-5 years in prison.

Good government is often used as tormentors. However, there are other less obvious tormentors at play like guilt, fear, depression, physical and emotional suffering, stress and so on.

The wicked servant was selfish. He wanted power and was willing to use anyone to get it. They are easy to identify in life. Stay away from them.

Be quick to forgive. You will save a lot of suffering in the long run….and remember, forgiveness is a two way street.

I think that we are to forgive in all conditions but the extent of the offense plays a big part in our *"After The Offense"* life.

Also, who is causing the offense makes a big difference on our plans for forgiving. A brother or sister in Christ is different than a stranger and the situation in which the offence occurs is a factor as well.

I am sure you have heard of the answer Jesus gave when asked about forgiveness. I call it the 70 X 7 Scenario.

"Then came Peter to him, and said, Lord, how oft shall my brother sin against me, and I forgive him? till seven times?... Jesus saith unto him, I say not unto thee, until seven times: but, until seventy times seven". Matthew 18:21-22

Note that Peter refers to a brother. Jesus says 70 X 7, which I believe, is a metaphor for an unlimited amount. This would be consistent with God's unlimited mercy. The fact that there is a clear repentance on the part of the offender indicates that the offender is seeking reconciliation.

I believe that repeated assaults by one individual would establish a pattern that is predictable. To extend unlimited mercy would be an act of God's love that transcends our human ability. The one being offended must above all else examine the motives and intent of the one causing the fault. Here's why:

The devil can use anyone to steal your joy and crush your spirit. If a brother or anyone else is continually offending you, there's got to be an underlying reason that needs to be dealt with.

Brothers and sisters in Christ, as well as family members, are close to you and can, if not corrected, dominate you with offensive actions that are meant to control you. That's not good.

It is not good for you or the offender to continue a relationship of offense and forgiveness. It will cause unwanted stress and anxiety.

Under What Conditions Do We Not Forgive?

There are no conditions in which we do not have to forgive. Jesus made that clear when He said, "Matthew 6:14-15:

"For if you forgive men when they sin against you, your heavenly Father will also forgive you. But if you do not forgive men their sins, your Father will not forgive your sins."

There are however a few conditions where it is not advisable to forgive without an apology. Let's look at them.

When the offender does not ask to be forgiven. If we forgive before they ask, we diminish the seriousness of the offense and suggest to the offender that we can be played or controlled by their oppression. Jesus said we were to forgive every time they ask.

When we stand up for what we believe. We, by standing up for what we believe, run the risk of offending others or being offended by others. To forgive in this situation can cause the offender to dismiss the premise of our stand and initiate further attacks.

Will God be mad at you for standing your ground against the attack of the devil that came through the offender? Peter told the early church,

"Be of sober spirit, be on the alert. Your adversary, the devil, prowls around like a roaring lion, seeking someone to devour. But resist him, firm in your faith, knowing that the same experiences of suffering are being accomplished by your brethren who are in the world" I Peter 5:8-9

God will not be angry. He tells us, in no uncertain terms, that we are to watch out for offenses that come our way as fiery darts.

The sad part is that often these darts are channeled through people. They are energized by attitudes of jealousy, envy and other fleshly emotions. It is important to remember who our enemy really is. It is not the offender.

"For we wrestle not against flesh and blood, but against principalities, against powers, against the rulers of the

darkness of this world, against spiritual wickedness in high places." Ephesians 6:12

Our real battle is with these evil entities that are bent on our destruction. They will use any human they can find to channel their lies. We, of course, need to avoid them or confront those who hurl the fiery darts of Satan and we are also empowered by the Holy Spirit to speak to these evil ones, in the name of Jesus, and bind them from further attacks and cast them out of our reality.

Matthew 6:14-15 is another key scripture on forgiveness. Verse 9-13 is where Jesus shares the Lord's Prayer. Then He says we need to forgive men their trespasses so our Heavenly Father can forgive us.

However, this does not mean we make every offender our bosom buddy. There are some folks that harbor hate towards you for lots of different reasons and will not even consider an apology. Yet others are too stubborn to initiate a discussion much less offer an apology.

We are still admonished by the scriptures to forgive them, even if we cannot reconcile. It's the only way to gain forgiveness from God. The offense is not the focal point of Jesus' teaching. The focal point is forgiveness because it mirrors the nature and will of God.

Confronting The Offender

"Then said he unto the disciples, it is impossible but that

offences will come: but woe [unto him], through whom they come! It were better for him that a millstone were hanged about his neck, and he cast into the sea, than that he should offend one of these little ones.

Take heed to yourselves: If thy brother trespass against thee, rebuke him; and if he repent, forgive him. And if he trespasses against thee seven times in a day, and seven times in a day turn again to thee, saying, I repent; thou shalt forgive him. Luke 17:3-4

Jesus made it clear that we are to confront the offender with a strong rebuke, showing him or her the error of his or her ways.

He also says this with regard to brethren, not strangers. However, he does warn us to, "Take Head" or watch carefully so you do not fall under the attacks of evil people.

With those in the community of Faith, we are to be ready to forgive when the offender repents. We are also encouraged to rebuke or express sharp disapproval or criticism of (someone) because of their behavior or actions.

Don't be afraid to challenge their authority and criticize them for their evil actions. I believe this is a good course of action for anyone that has been offended.

Dealing With Play Actors

I have had several encounters where my offenders were play acting as in a movie, living out a role, so as to deceive me into thinking he wanted forgiveness but I could see it was clearly an act.

Sincerity is essential in the giving and acceptance of forgiveness. That's because healing from God is transmitted from one to the other and it is not a joke. Take the habitual drunk that begs for forgiveness but never follows through. This is a prime example of what I am saying here.

There must be guidelines to giving forgiveness in cases like this…things like attending AA or getting professional counseling, etc. Also, in the case of adultery, it is a break in trust and some borders or guidelines must be established to insure sincerity.

Denial Is Not Forgiveness

The inability to really forgive is often due to a false concept that "forgetting is forgiving". Forgetting is NOT forgiving. To be sure, if we forgive we will forget as a result. But the reverse is not true: forgetting is not forgiving--it is denial.

Ps 51:6 *Behold, thou desires truth in the inward parts: and in the hidden part thou shalt make me to know wisdom.*

If we attempt to achieve a bogus forgiveness by deliberately putting the offence "out of mind" we might be fooling ourselves and others that we have "forgiven". But all of the emotions and plots and hurt are still there, only held back by force of will in a deliberate denial.

But when we see "that person" again all the bitterness and pain could rise up again within us. Or, in the off moment, when such mental gymnastics cannot be maintained, we catch ourselves in an elaborate meditation of revenge or fit of rage and anger.

Then we see just how deep and effective this sort of "forgiveness" is. A mind "bent" by denial has a nasty habit of "snapping back" in the worst of moments.

"Any one who professes to be in the light and yet hates his brother is still in darkness." 1 John 2:9

Denial is merely a delusion: flimsy, fake, and shallow. Forgiveness is real: robust and solid. It is not an avoiding of the truth, but a specific dealing with it squarely, however painful. Consider God's perspective.

Nothing is hidden from His sight: the evil intent, the hidden lust, the damage done, the choosing of that which is wrong, etc. And yet He is the author and originator of forgiveness.

If we are going to really forgive, we are going to have to do it God's way: with our eyes open. For those God chooses to forgive, He will "forget" their sins, "remembering them no more". But let us not accuse the omniscient God of not knowing something or of being ignorant of any fact.

He has told us that nothing is beyond His sight. Rather let us understand the "figure of speech" and spiritual dynamic of how God forgives.

Heb 8:12 (NIV) *"For I will forgive their wickedness and will remember their sins no more."*

The order here is essential. Forgiveness first, forget is second. Until real forgiveness takes place, the offense is "in our faces" as regards that person, and it is the same with God. The sin comes between us, and cannot be "forgotten" until dealt with.

If and when we enter into true forgiveness, we can then regard the person without the "offense" looming first and foremost between us.

Isa. 43:25 (NIV) *"I, even I, am he who blots out your transgressions, for my own sake, and remembers your sins no more.*

CHAPTER FIVE

No Obvious Reason

Sometimes we suffer and don't know why. Why am I suffering so? We tend to rehearse all the positive things that identify us as a good person and thus worthy of good health and emotional stability. Our cry is, "I didn't do anything wrong."

When there is no apparent reason for our discomfort, we can still have victory and peace of mind. It is not always necessary to know why. What is important is that we know what to do to overcome the suffering or to deal with it.

As long as we know deep within that we are right with God, we can trust Him to make things better. If He is Lord over my life instead of me, I can rest assured that He will be there to help me get through whatever I am facing. Here's a scripture to remember.

"And we know that all things work together for good to them that love God, to them who are the called according to his purpose." Romans 8:28

This is a promise that we can hook our faith on. We don't know when. We don't know how. But we do know He is there, working everything together for our good.

The question is, are you called according to his purposes? Are you demonstrating love towards God?

We are all called out of darkness to walk in the light of God's glory. Romans 8:29-30, Our destiny and His purpose is to transform us into the image of His dear Son.

So, we all who have been, "Born Again" are eligible to receive the promise. He will work everything together for good.

When the reason for our suffering is not apparent, we are to hold fast to the promises of God and believe them with all of our hearts. It's called having faith. The reason will be revealed in due time if we faint not.

I know that there will be some that disagree with my rationale, saying, "I believed and still suffered…nothing happened."

What do you do when you pray and believe and nothing happens? That's simple, you keep on keeping on. When you have done all you can do to stand in faith, you then stand and believe, no matter what.

Realize that we are talking about being delivered from suffering…not getting a new car for Christmas or winning the Loto. Those things are probably not in God's will.

However, being in good health is.

"Beloved, I wish above all things that thou may prosper and be in health, even as thy soul prosper." 3 John verse 2

Jesus put it this way,

"The thief comes not, but for to steal, and to kill, and to destroy: I am come that they might have life, and that they might have it more abundantly." John 10:10

Let's not forget man's free will and the consequences of those decisions. Sometimes our actions produce an alternate reality where pain and suffering exist. The smoker that suddenly has cancer knows it well. The alcoholic that totals his or her car and is crippled for life also knows it well.

Our decisions can alter our reality and produce a lifestyle of suffering and pain. In such cases, it is easy to forget the reason we are now suffering. Many blame others instead of themselves.

The point is, when we do not know why, don't labor over it. God will show you why in His timing and the pathway to healing or victory.

Your job is to pray and seek the Lord for revelation knowledge as to what to do next.

The apostle Paul did this. Hear what happened when Paul sought the Lord about a thorn in his side.

"For this thing I besought the Lord thrice, that it might de-

part from me. And he said unto me, My grace is sufficient for thee: for my strength is made perfect in weakness. Most gladly therefore will I rather glory in my infirmities, that the power of Christ may rest upon me.

Therefore I take pleasure in infirmities, in reproaches, in necessities, in persecutions, in distresses for Christ's sake: for when I am weak, then am I strong." 2 Corinthians 12:8-10

It is believed that the thorn in Paul's side was a group of Jews that followed him everywhere and tried to discredit his ministry. What ever it was, God said that His grace was all that Paul needed. Paul's conclusion was to glory in his suffering that the name of Jesus would be magnified.

When we stop crying and complaining about what we are going through we can glory in our suffering knowing that God's grace will see us through and give us all the strength we need. His power is manifested in our weakness.

Finally, when there is no obvious reason for your suffering, try this scripture on for size. It is a clear answer when the reason is not obvious.

"Yea, and all that will live godly in Christ Jesus shall <u>suffer</u> persecution." 2 Timothy 2:12

CHAPTER SIX

Religious Persecution

We can suffer as a result of our faith. What we believe can hurt us. Here's what the Bible says:

"yea, and all that will live godly in Christ Jesus shall suffer persecution. But evil men and seducers shall wax worse and worse, deceiving, and being deceived. But continue thou in the things which thou hast learned and hast been assured of, knowing of whom thou hast learned them" 2 Timothy 3:12-14

They never told me that if I really got serious in following Jesus that I would suffer persecution. I found that out the hard way, by striving to live a Godly life.

I quickly discovered evil forces at work to cause me to slack off and be more liberal in my thinking. You know, to embrace abortion, take a drink now and then, tell a dirty joke, and frequent a local bar with like-minded friends.

What really shocked me was when I saw those evil forces

at work in my family, my friends, church folks and co-workers. They all were concerned that I night get too fanatic and go off the deep end. All I wanted to do was walk with Jesus and be a blessing to my Heavenly Father.

I guess the deep end was walking in the Spirit instead of the flesh as they were doing. Their expectations became a thorn in my side and the source of much suffering. I lost friends, backed away from church and became distant. I stood at arm's length. It was the only way for me to move on with God.

Arms Length

I hold the world at arm's length
That their choices may not interfere.
While they do their own thing,
I watch and wait over here.

My steps must not go their way
For it's not where I need to be.
The Lord has shown me the path
That will lead me to my destiny.

The call to follow them is strong
And pulls at me now and then.
But I know with-in my heart
That their way is full of sin.

I must move on in life
Beyond their beckoning call.
It's the right thing to do,
So I do not stumble or fall.

I will not be swayed
By family, friends or business deal.
Their secret thoughts are not mine
To consider, to admire or feel.

So I keep the world at arm's length
As I journey through this life.
My faith in Jesus will keep me strong
As I walk in His glorious light.

Poem By
John Marinelli

To live Godly in Christ Jesus is not to adhere to a set of rules and regulations or church doctrine. Living Godly is to live like God. How does He live? He lives as the eternal Spirit. His character is exampled in the scriptures. It is referred to as the fruit of the Spirit.

"But the fruit of the Spirit is love, joy, peace, longsuffering, gentleness, goodness, faith, Meekness, temperance: against such there is no law." Galatians 5:22

Living Godly is to walk in these attributes. They should paint a word picture of God in and through your personality. That is being like God, His image and likeness on the earth. That is allowing your light to shine. That is how you walk in the Spirit.

Guess what? There are more than 3,000 Christian sects/denominations in this world. They all strive to capture followers offering various doctrines that appeal to religious needs. Many are heretical and are down right false. Their doctrines shut up the kingdom of God instead of opening it to the masses.

The true test is in the application of John 3:16

"For God so loved the world, that he gave his only begotten Son, that whosoever believeth in him should not perish, but have everlasting life."

The kingdom of God is open to all the, "Whosoevers" of John 3:16. It is not restricted to just one religion of group. There is no "true church." We are all called of God to mirror His image and likeness in the earth. We are the, "Whosoevers."

It is the church fighting among itself that causes most of the religious persecution. We must stand against false doctrines and heretical teachings.

It's time to stand up and tell the world that we are "Whosoever" Christians that have believed on Jesus and now walk in the Spirit of the living God. Don't be afraid to share your faith and belief in Christ. It is why you are here in this generation and at this time.

The infighting of the church is not the only source of religious persecution. Other religions also hate Christians. They abuse and attack believers for trusting in Christ. Some countries even hold a death sentence over the believer's head. (Eleven Christians are killed every day for believing in Christ.)

Back in the 60s I supported a secret group that smuggled bibles into Russia. They printed the bibles in the Russian language and sent them behind the, "Iron Curtain."

The church was underground, hiding from the authorities. Some pastors were caught and tossed into prison just for worshiping God.

Then there is the ungodly that attack the Godly because of their faith. They push secularism and evolution, teaching it in our schools and pushing it into law with the full support of the government.

All of this is a coordinated attack on the faith of the believer designed to crush your core belief system and persuade you to become like them. The apostle Peter put it this way:

"Be sober, be vigilant; because your adversary the devil, as a roaring lion, walketh about, seeking whom he may devour: Whom resist stedfast in the faith, knowing that the same afflictions are accomplished in your brethren that are in the world." I Peter 5:8-9

Being sober, as Peter suggest, is the same as being street smart. You stay keenly aware of your circumstances; ever watching to be sure you don't get caught up in a trap of the devil.

CHAPTER SEVEN

Demonic Attacks & Suffering

Demonic attacks are somewhat different than other reasons behind the suffering of the righteous.

So far, we have been discussing the hate and jealousy of people and their quest to have power over you. Now we will be discussing the attacks of the devil and how they can cause suffering.

In chapter six I called attention to Peter's warning to the church. Here it is again:

"Be sober, be vigilant; because your adversary the devil, as a roaring lion, walks about, seeking whom he may devour: Whom resist stedfast in the faith, knowing that the same afflictions are accomplished in your brethren that are in the world." I Peter 5:8-9

There is some good news so don't get too depressed.

First, *The battle is the Lord's.*

" Thus saith the Lord unto you, be not afraid nor dismayed by reason of this great multitude; for the battle is not yours, but God's." II Chronicles 20:15 God wants us to know that He has everything under control.

Second, *God has given us His armour to wear so we don't get hurt.*

"Finally, my brethren, be strong in the Lord, and in the power of his might. Put on the whole armor of God, that ye may be able to stand against the wiles of the devil.

For we wrestle not against flesh and blood, but against principalities, against powers, against the rulers of the darkness of this world, against spiritual wickedness in high places. Ephesians 6:10-18

Third, *Jesus has already defeated every evil power.*

"And having spoiled principalities and powers, He made a show of them openly, triumphing over them in it." Colossians 2:15

The victory was at the cross where He died as a sacrifice for sin.

"For what the law could not do, in that it was weak through the flesh, God sending his own Son in the likeness

of sinful flesh, and for sin, condemned sin in the flesh:" Romans 8:3

Finally, God wants us to walk in the Spirit so we do not fulfill the deeds of the flesh.

"This I say then, Walk in the Spirit, and ye shall not fulfill the lust of the flesh." Galatians 5:16

The deeds of the flesh are listed in Galatians, chapter five. It is the flesh that causes us all the problems.

It is important to know that Satan's authority and powers were taken away. He must steal power from human beings to operate. He does this through deception, intimidation and fear.

The battle rages on in the earth but now it is in our minds. Evil spirits are continually planting thoughts in our minds that, if entertained, will take us to a place of fear where we are tormented.

These evil thoughts are like fiery darts that pierce our souls and cause emotional trauma and even physical sickness.

The enemy can easily create an illusion, movie quality, of bad things from the past or begin a lengthy attack of critical comments that are meant to wear you down and get you to think about the hurt you felt back in days now gone by.

Satan always tells lies to deceive us. If we buy the lie, we live out that destiny. If, on the other hand, we know the truth, it will set us free to shape our own destiny in accordance with God's will.

Knowing the truth is the greatest weapon we can have and use against evil influences. If you are not sure of what is truth, read the Bible. It is full of God's Word. Here's an example of how to use it to defeat Satan.

Evil is the hour of temptation when Satan seeks to deceive us and draw us away from God. It is also when fiery darts are flung at us by demons.

The deceptions are suggestive thoughts that are always contrary to God's will but seem logical such as, "everybody's doing it. Therefore it must be ok" or "drugs can't really hurt you." The fiery darts are insults like, "You're not good enough", "Not worth anything", "Never amount to anything"…all are negative and are meant to cause a low self-esteem, depression and even suicide.

The Sword of the Spirit is really cool because it's fashioned from over 3,000 promises of God…things like;

"You are accepted in the beloved" Ephesians 1:6,

"I am crucified with Christ: nevertheless I live; yet not I, but Christ lives in me: and the life which I now live in the flesh I live by the faith of the Son of God, who loved me, and gave himself for me." Galatians 2:20"

"Nay, in all these things we are more than conquerors through him that loved us." Romans 8:37

All of Satan's efforts are designed to establish strongholds in our lives. How many has he established in you?

What's a stronghold? Try these on for size: Over-eating, drugs, smoking, anger, homosexuality, pornography, and all of the deeds of the flesh listed in Galatians chapter five. He'll try and try until he gets you hooked on some sort of vice.

If you follow him, he'll take you deeper and deeper until a stronghold is built which is really an outpost for demonic activity.

Not to worry because the Sword of the Spirit can cut that evil stronghold into pieces and bring its efforts to naught.

Battling evil spirits that invade our minds and try to get us to surrender our authority is a full time job. It takes a continual awareness and a good knowledge of the Word of God.

When was he last time you worried? Do you get fearful when things go wrong? Most of us dwell on things that we cannot change and suffer emotional stress through it all.

Stress can kill you. It is a byproduct of worry or being anxious. However, if you know that what you are feeling is only evil spirits roaring like lions, you can quench their fiery darts with scriptural promises before they hit your soul.

The same evil spirits have no authority to do anything to you unless you buy their lies and dwell on their thoughts.

That's why Peter said, Be Sober! Be Vigilant! He tells the church because they can get attacked at anytime in any situation.

If you are suffering from emotional trauma, stress or even physical ailments, seek the Lord in prayer and stand against every attack with the promises of God.

Here's what Paul wrote to the church of the 1st century:

"And bringing into captivity every thought to the obedience of Christ;" II Corinthians 10:5

Note: we are to bring every thought into captivity. In other words…hold every thought against the truth of the Word of God to be sure it is not a deception or trap. Your obedience to the truth will keep you free.

Little Prisons

Little prisons await
the lustful soul.
Bars of selfishness and pride
create dungeons of icy cold.

Prisons of shame and jealousy
fill the heart with utter despair.
Bars that separate from God
and those that really care.

Stand back!
While the doors
are tightly closed,
sealing away your life,
to wither as a dying rose.

Beware of those little prisons
that trap the lustful soul.
Keep yourself free from sin,
thru faith in the Christ of old.

Poem By
John Marinelli

CHAPTER EIGHT

False Doctrines & Suffering

A doctrine is a belief or set of beliefs held and taught by a church, political party, or other group. If that doctrine is false it can destroy lives and lead seekers of truth into darkness.

Is what you believe true or false? If it is false it is nothing more than a lie. When you believe a lie, you fall under its spell and into an alternate reality.

Today's religious world is full of false doctrines that began as lies designed to deceive and lead believers astray. They appeared on the scene in the 1st century and still exist today.

The Mormons, Jehovah's Witness and Christian Science are all centered in false doctrines. I am sure you will see more as we continue. They have embraced doctrines of devils.

The only way to know if a doctrine is false is to know the

truth. Then you can hold every doctrine up to the truth and see if it is true or false.

Jesus said, *"Take heed therefore that the light which is in thee be not darkness."* Luke 11:35

I have run across many folks that called themselves Christian but followed false teaching. They suffered under the leadership of false teachers that kept them in darkness. They claimed to be walking in the light but what they believed was not what the Bible taught. Many were half truth and half error so as to make the unlearned think that it was all true.

Even mainstream churches strayed off the true path to follow false teachings. Let me show you some examples.

One doctrine that is central to Christianity is that Jesus was born of a virgin. According to the PEW report on religion, 34% of all U.S. adults don't believe in the virgin birth.

Here are more shocking statistics:

1. 52% of all "Christians" believe that non-Christian faiths can lead to eternal life. But the Bible says, *"Neither is there salvation in any other: for there is none other name under heaven given among men, whereby we must be saved."* Acts 4:12 (See also John 3:16)

2. 65% of Americans believe that even though everyone sins that people are still good by nature. However the Bible says, "As it is written, there

is none righteous, no, not one: *There is none that understandeth, there is none that seeketh after God. They are all gone out of the way, they are together become unprofitable; there is none that doeth good, no, not one."* Romans 3-10-12

3. 77% of all Americans believe that personal salvation is through good works. The Bible says otherwise.

"For by grace are ye saved through faith; and that not of yourselves: it is the gift of God: Not of works, lest any man should boast."

Ephesians2:8-9

If you are confused, read your Bible. The Holy Spirit of God will lead you into all truth. He will show you the way.

There are many false teachers and many false doctrines that claim to have the truth. Don't believe them without first searching the scriptures to be sure that what they are saying is in line with what the Bible teaches. They are anti-Christ.

Here's what Paul said,

"But though we, or an angel from heaven, preach any other gospel unto you than that which we have preached unto you, let him be accursed. As we said before, so say I now again, if any man preach any other gospel unto you

than that ye have received, let him be accursed." Galatians 1:8-9

Lies, or false doctrines are very dangerous. They can strip you of your core values and keep you in bondage to a false reality that is anti-Christ. Know the scripture and use it to dispel the lies.

"All scripture is given by inspiration of God, and is profitable for doctrine, for reproof, for correction, for instruction in righteousness: That the man of God may be perfect, thoroughly furnished unto all good works." 2 Timothy 3:16-17

CHAPTER NINE

A Lack of Knowledge & Suffering

The Bible says,

"*My people are destroyed for lack of knowledge: because thou hast rejected knowledge, I will also reject thee, that thou shalt be no priest to me: seeing thou hast forgotten the law of thy God, I will also forget thy children.*: Hosea 4:6

We are all kings and priest unto the most high God.

"*And hath made us kings and priests unto God and his Father; to him be glory and dominion for ever and ever. Amen.*" Revelation 1:6

We do not want to reject the knowledge of God for it is what keeps us free. Yet more than half of Christians today do not read their Bible and are not trained in spiritual warfare.

How can we stay free if we neglect our only source of power? The psalmist said,

"Thy word have I hid in mine heart, that I might not sin against thee." Psalm 118:11

The righteous suffer when they neglect the promises of God. They fall from the grace of God and are destroyed.

I do not mean to imply that they lose their salvation. I do mean that they surrender their power to evil forces and that leaves them open for demonic attacks and destruction.

God expects us to fight the good fight of faith… to resist evil, deny the flesh and to walk in His Spirit.

How can we lose what God has set in place for our benefit? It can only happen if we ignore the only source of power available to us? Our lack of knowledge will cause great suffering at the hands of Satan.

"Study to shew thyself approved unto God, a workman that needeth not to be ashamed, rightly dividing the word of truth." 2 Timothy 2:15

"If I don't know, I cannot be held accountable." That is what some of my friends tell me. The problem is…God holds us accountable for every idle word and deed. Listen to this:

"For God shall bring every work into judgment, with every secret thing, whether it be good, or whether it be evil."
"But I say unto you, That every idle word that men shall speak, they shall give account thereof in the day of judgment." Matthew 12:36

"So then every one of us shall give account of himself to God." Romans 14:12

Get the point? We cannot go through life and stay ignorant of the will of God. He will not allow it. If we close our eyes and shut our mouths, we will stand before God and give an account.

There is no neutrality. Jesus said,

"He that is not with me is against me; and he that gathereth not with me scattereth abroad. Either make the tree good, and his fruit good; or else make the tree corrupt, and his fruit corrupt: for the tree is known by his fruit." Matthew 12:30 & 33

When we invited Jesus into our hearts, we ask Him to save our souls and be our Lord. That means He rules and His will is supreme. That means we are with Him and willing to follow His lead.

This is what makes Christianity so great. We actually communicate with our Savior and obey His directives, knowing He has our best interest at heart.

Your current suffering could be because you do not know that you do not have to suffer. Therefore, you do not apply scripture to the situation that is causing you to suffer. You just suffer in silence or in a loud voice of desperation.

The better thing to do is to learn all you can and apply it as often as needed so you do not fall into darkness. Look for the Lighthouse.

The Lighthouse

A lighthouse is a blessing,
To the ships that toss in the sea,
For it shows them the way,
Until they can clearly see.

The rage of an angry storm
cannot hide its brilliant light.
Nor can its awesome furry,
Rule as an endless night.

Jesus is the lighthouse,
for those who have gone astray.
The light of His love,
Offers a new and living way.

Jesus is the lighthouse,
When fear and sickness rage.
The light of His love,
Gives hope in difficult days.

So trust in the Lord,
and look for His light.
He alone is "The Lighthouse",
that guides you through the night.

Poem By
John Marinelli

CHAPTER TEN

True Lies & Suffering

Sometimes we hear something so often that we start to accept it as factual and believe it as being true. That's how false data is presented as fact. I call this "True Lies."

Here's an example of false data that is now taught in our schools and promoted as scientific fact. *I am talking about Evolution.*

For those of us that may not know what evolution is, it is the process by which different kinds of living organisms are thought to have developed and diversified from earlier forms.

It is the gradual development of something, from a simple to a more complex form.

Darwin's theory, over the years, has become fact, accepted in all walks of life and even in the scientific community. It also includes man as one of the living organisms that evolved.

This theory is, of course, contrary to the Bible and it eliminates God, as the creator of all living things.

It's premise is that if you apply enough time, existing chemicals and other substances will come together and, life will spark to form living organisms that over more time will grow and develop into higher organisms and eventually plant, animal and even human life.

That's like saying if I place all the raw materials needed to make a watch in a bucket and leave it for millions of years it will eventually become a fully operational watch. Time and substances cannot produce life.

Nevertheless, this lie is now accepted as truth and it has destroyed thousands of lives as a result. Here's why:

1. The theory leaves out God. It is the atheist's way of denying God.

2. It says to our youth, "you have no purpose in life. All you can look forward to is death."

3. Life has no meaning or value.

4. Why strive to achieve. There is no point to it or lasting reward.

According to Emile Borel, a French scientist and expert in the area of probability, an event on the cosmic level with a probability of less than 1 out of 10, to the 50th power, will not happen. The probability of producing one human cell by chance is 10, to the 119,000 power. It's just not possible.

Again, the Bible is the only source for a realistic understanding of life. I will point to "Intelligent Design" as a proof text that God was and is still behind the creation of all things including man.

This, "True Lie" has fostered depression, hopelessness and suicide. Believe the lie and you too will suffer, even though you are among the righteous.

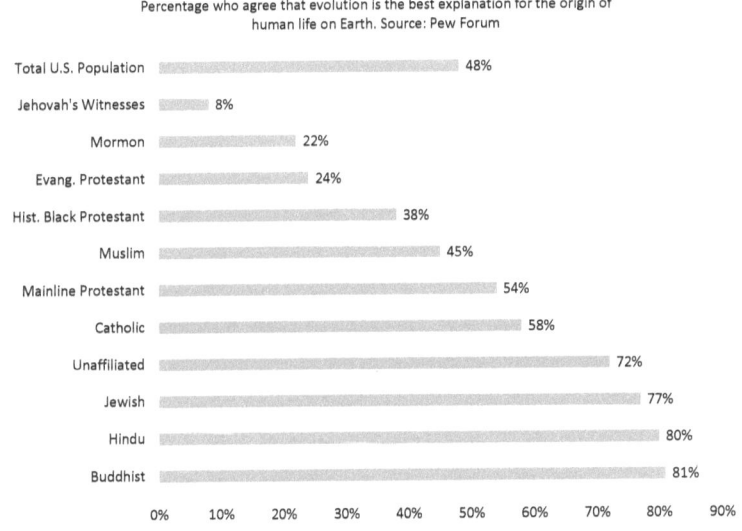

Did you see that? 48% of the U. S. Population believes that evolution is true. Look at all the Christians. 58 % are Catholic, 51% are mainline protestant and 77% are Jewish, God's chosen people. They all are trapped in this "True Lie" scenario.

The above survey was conducted in 2007. It is now 14 years old. Here's how it looks in 2020.

According to the *Pew Research* Center, 62 percent of adults in the United States *accept* human *evolution* while 34 percent of adults *believe* that humans have always existed in their present form.

Where do you stand? Are you caught in a, "True Lie." If you are, go back to the Bible and read Genesis and see God at work as He creates man in His own image and likeness.

CHAPTER ELEVEN

False Assumptions & Suffering

When we assume that a certain thing is true when it is really not, we end up drawing erroneous conclusions, which, if not corrected, can cause us to easily fall into error.

The righteous often suffer because they jump to conclusions without first investigating the situation to check the facts. That's how gossip starts and reputations are destroyed.

Again, the Bible gives us some direction. Check it out.

"Man looks on the outward appearance but the Lord looks at the heart." I Samuel 16:7

What you see on the outward appearance is not always what is going on inside the heart. We need to be careful about making judgments. We can become an agent of persecution against another brother or sister in Christ. That's what the devil wants.

"Therefore judge nothing before the time, until the Lord

come, who both will bring to light the hidden things of darkness, and will make manifest the counsels of the hearts: and then shall every man have praise of God." I Corinthians 4:5

That means we must, above all things, get rid of our critical spirits. They are an extension of Satan's personality. They are meant to manifest the image and likeness of evil.

Here's what William Ekstrum of the University of Louisiana has to say about assumptions.

An assumption is an unexamined belief: what we think without realizing we think it. Our inferences (also called conclusions) are often based on assumptions that we haven't thought about critically.

A critical thinker, however, is attentive to these assumptions because they are sometimes incorrect or misguided. Just because we assume something is true doesn't mean it is.

Think carefully about your assumptions when finding and analyzing information but also think carefully about the assumptions of others.

Whether you're looking at a website or a scholarly article, you should always consider the author's assumptions. Are the author's conclusions based on assumptions that she or he hasn't thought about logically?

Sarah Blick, from Thrive Global, offers nine reasons why we should avoid making assumptions.

1. **They're an easy out.**

The path of least resistance is also the path of least growth.

2. **They stop you from taking responsibility for your life.**

Assumptions allow you to hide behind your version of the story. This means you don't own your part in the true story. You prefer to blame others for your misfortune, rather than look in the mirror.

3. **They keep you stuck in the past.**

Assumptions rely on old information to fill in blanks and connect dots. Instead of expanding your horizons, you retreat into the past.

4. **It's lazy behavior.**

Instead of asking questions to get the information you need, you jump to conclusions.

5. **They foster a negative mindset.**

Most assumptions are derived from old, painful information. This reinforces your innate negativity bias.

6. **It's toxic behavior.**

To protect yourself from more hurt, you use your

assumptions to lash out at others. This is bad for them, and you.

7. They become a bad habit.

The more you make assumptions, the easier it is to continue making them.

8. They deepen your pain.

The more you pick at a sore, the more painful it gets and it doesn't get a chance to heal.

9. Assumptions are ALWAYS wrong.

I have a perfect record with the assumptions I've made. 100% of them have been wrong. And it's hard to believe that I'm unique in this.

If you are the victim of false assumptions you have two choices as to what to do. You can forget about it, considering the source…that those who make false assumptions against you are idiots or you can fight back by confronting them all with the truth.

However, those that make judgments against you that are not founded in the truth will most likely reject what you tell them. They have already made their judgments and assumptions…. Good luck with that.

CHAPTER TWELVE

Not knowing God's Will

Suffering also happens to the righteous because they are ignorant of Biblical truth. They usually are too busy living for themselves. They strive to get ahead but are unaware of the Biblical principles that ensure success.

Because they are ignorant of the promises of God, they have no idea what His will is for them. Not knowing God's will causes confusion. Then comes anxiety, fear, worry and torment.

What do you do when trouble comes your way? You'll recall we discussed this earlier.

"Yea, and all that will live godly in Christ Jesus shall suffer persecution." 2 Timothy 3:12

When this persecution knocks at your door, what do you do? Here's a multiple-choice quiz:

    1. Run away and hide.

    2. Cry on a friend's shoulder.

3. Suffer in silence.

If the above three possibilities do not fit, how do you find God's Will for your life?

When I was a young Christian, I wished with all my heart that I could actually know the will of God. I often sent up prayers to heaven saying, "Lord, what do I do now?" It got so bad that I could hardly drive my car because I couldn't decide if God wanted me in the left or right lane.

Months went by with my continual prayers to God that shouted into heaven, "What Do I Do Now?" Finally, I was invited to a Bible study, started going to church and began reading my Bible.

The answers came ever so slow but fast enough for me to digest and store them away in my heart.

Now, after 50+ years of Bible study, prayer and life-application, I can say with confidence that I do know and understand "God's Will" for my life.

I am still learning and studying and applying. I even, at times, ask my self, "Why didn't I see that before now?

There is a way to "know that you know" so there is no more doubt. However, knowing that you know takes Faith.

God is speaking all the time through the Bible, through His Spirit and through other folks that He brings into your life. You just need to calm down and listen.

The quick fix to "Knowing That You Know" is to "Listen

And Believe." To know that you know is a great feeling because there is no anxiety in it. I know and have been persuaded that this way is the right way and my new perspective brings me a lot of comfort, peace and hope for the future.

"And thine ears shall hear a word behind thee, saying, this is the way, walk ye in it, when ye turn to the right hand, and when ye turn to the left." Isaiah 30:21

The Bible says,

"For ye have not received the spirit of bondage again to fear; but ye have received the Spirit of adoption, whereby we cry, Abba, Father. The Spirit itself beareth witness with our spirit, that we are the children of God: And if children, then heirs; heirs of God, and joint-heirs with Christ; if so be that we suffer with him, that we may be also glorified together." Romans 8:15- 17

As the scripture says, the Spirit of God will bear witness with our spirits that we are the children of God. If you've ever felt, seen or otherwise realized the witness of God's Spirit, you will know without a shadow of a doubt that you are a child of God…. and if a child also a joint heir with Christ.

Notice that the apostle Paul didn't say that the Spirit bears witness with our flesh, our souls or minds. He didn't say the witness would be through the intellect.

He said the witness would be from Spirit to spirit. That

means it could be one of many gentle quiet assurances that we did the right thing at the right time.

It could be a sense of stability when things are going rough. It could be, an "I just know" feeling.

The point here is that God's Spirit is talking to us and our spirit is listening and rejoicing that it can hear God when He speaks.

One definite witness, that I can recall, is when I read the scriptures they started jumping off the page with new and fresh revelation.

The Bible, all of a sudden, came alive and spoke directly to my spirit. God's Holy Spirit was and is still confirming to me that I am a child of the Living God.

So we have a quiet assurance and a loud voice that calls us to the Word of God, where we receive faith, instruction, assurance, strength, knowledge and a lot more. God's witness is everywhere.

Finding God's Will is not rocket science. We have already learned that God's Holy Spirit is available to confirm or excuse our decisions in life.

We also know that it is our," Free Will" that engages truth and activates faith to empower us to walk in the Spirit.

The key to "Knowing That You Know" is absolute submission to His Will. Here's what Jesus said,

"If any man will do his will, (God's Will), he shall know of

the doctrine, whether it be of God, or whether I speak of myself." John 17:7

We have to be ready and willing to do His Will. When we are, we will know the doctrine or revelation knowledge necessary to accomplish the revealed Will of God.

Question! Why should God give us the knowledge of His Will if we are not willing or not ready to use it? That would be a waste of time and energy on God's part and He just doesn't operate that way. He has, however, already revealed His Will in the pages of the Bible.

The best way to find God's Will for your life is not to ask friends, family, or anyone else. They are not God and often are wrong in their own decisions, which, if I am right, will show up in their lives as a testimony against them.

The best way to know God's Will is to ask God in prayer, stay in the Bible and look for direction, correction and guidance. It's all there. If you start a log of scripture verses and what they specifically meant to you, you'll have a history to refer to when you feel lost or confused.

Whatever you do, don't become idle and neglect the things of God.

God is waiting for you to decide. Your life on this earth and your eternal destiny is at stake.

CONCLUSION

Why do the righteous suffer? The answer is clear.

"Yea, and all that will live godly in Christ Jesus shall suffer persecution." 2 Timothy 2:12

We are marked for suffering by evil forces because we live godly in Christ Jesus. That suffering comes in various forms. There is only one single reason we can point to and say, "This is why."

We only know for sure that we will suffer persecution because we strive to live godly in Christ Jesus. We also know that God will deliver us from them all.

"Many are the afflictions of the righteous: but the Lord delivers him out of them all."

Nevertheless, there are indicators we can look to and draw conclusions. Living godly is one of them.

However, it also happens because of our bad "Free Will" choices. It happens when we disobey God. It happens as part of the divine providence of God. It happens because of an unforgiving heart.

It happens as a result of religious persecution. It happens as a result of demonic attacks. It happens as a result of false doctrine. It happens because of a lack of knowledge. It happens as a result of lies that are presented as truth. It happens as a result of false assumptions.

It happens because of not knowing God's will. It happens sometimes for no obvious reason.

Some are self-induced while others are a result of outside influences. We should not be so concerned about the "Why" but rather concentrate on the solution.

I am sure you will discover more reasons why the righteous suffers. I have presented twelve reasons so you have a basic working knowledge as to the "Why." If one of these reasons fits you, make the necessary adjustments and move on with God.

Here's a challenge for you from the apostle Paul. He gave up trying to figure it all out and…well read it for yourself.

"And I count all things but loss for the excellency of the knowledge of Christ Jesus my Lord: for whom I have suffered the loss of all things, and do count them but dung, that I may win Christ, and be found in him, not having mine own righteousness, which is of the law, but that which is through the faith of Christ, the righteousness which is of God by faith:

That I may know him, and the power of his resurrection,

and the fellowship of his sufferings, being made conformable unto his death;

If by any means I might attain unto the resurrection of the dead. Not as though I had already attained, either were already perfect: but I follow after, if that I may apprehend that for which also I am apprehended of Christ Jesus.

Brethren, I count not myself to have apprehended: but this one thing I do, forgetting those things which are behind, and reaching forth unto those things which are before, I press toward the mark for the prize of the high calling of God in Christ Jesus. Philippians 3:8-14

Your mission or challenge, should you accept it, is to be like Paul; to press toward the mark for the prize of the high calling of God in Christ Jesus and to forget those things which are behind, and reach forth unto those things which are before you.

When we are all entangled in the things of the past, we cannot be focused on what God wants for us now or in the future. We must forget the hurts and suffering of yesterday and press on towards our destiny in God.

The Steps of A Good Man

The steps of a good man
Are ordered by the Lord.
He leads us by still waters
Until our souls are restored.

Our pain and suffering
Are all taken away.
Replaced with real hope
For a brand new day.

He orders our steps
By Holy Spirit's breath,
That we may overcome
Satan, Sin and Death.

The steps of a good man,
Are not entirely his own.
They're given by God
So he doesn't walk alone.
Psalm 73:23

Written By
Rev. John Marinelli

ABOUT THE AUTHOR

John Marinelli

John Marinelli is an ordained Christian minister. He is the author of several other books, "The Art of Writing Christian Poetry", "Original Story Poems," a children's book, "Mysteries & Miracles," "Moonlight & Mistletoe", "With Eagle's Wings" which are Christian Fiction stories and "Pulpit Poems," a collection of over 250 Christian Poems for use by pastors and teachers, "The Believer's Handbook of Battle Strategies." And "How To Live A Victorious Christian Life" which is coming soon.

John has authored several one act plays and monologues that were marketed through Russell House Publishing to churches nationwide for use in their performance ministries.

He is also a dedicated Christian poet with award winning poems, some of which are permanently displayed on 3' X 4' billboards in Holy Land USA, a 250 acre nature park in Bedford, VA. Several other poems are framed and displayed at the Christian Church Conference Center is Silver Springs, Florida.

He has appeared with his wife, Marilyn on several TV programs including Trinity Broadcasting Network in Jacksonville Beach and Miami, Florida, as well as, numerous radio station interviews around the country.

He is now retired and living in central Florida where he continues to write and publish Christian related materials.

www.christianliferesourcecenter.org

www.ingramcontent.com/pod-product-compliance
Lightning Source LLC
Chambersburg PA
CBHW020429010526
44118CB00010B/499